MITT ROMNEY

The Biography of Mitt Romney

University Press

CONTENTS

PROLOGUE

Without question, it was the most difficult decision that Mitt Romney had ever had to make in his entire life.

More difficult than which direction his career should take – more difficult than the breathtaking choice of throwing his hat into the ring as a presidential candidate, not once, but twice. More difficult than packing up his suitcase to move to a foreign country for years, not knowing when he would see his family again. More difficult than stepping down from a position that meant everything to him, for what he hoped was the greater good.

He didn't want to go through with it; it terrified him. But he had no other options left.

Already, he'd heard the backlash from those who were meant to be his colleagues, his supporters. Strangers howling, "You ought to be ashamed of yourself!" in public places. A car driving by as he walked with his wife, the window rolling down. *"Traitor!"* The anger of the public was even more unsettling than that of the men and women who sat around him on the floor of the Senate. The other members of his party turned cold and judgmental, loud in their fury – and this was almost worse, quietly in agreement but too dedicated to the party line to speak up in his support.

Decades before, Romney had called himself an independent.

Now, preparing to stand alone as the first senator ever to vote to impeach a member of his own party, he was reminded of just what being truly independent meant.

Stand with the president, he had been told over and over for the past four years. *Don't let the party down.*

Regardless of what he says and does? Romney had asked them. *Regardless of his point of view? Regardless of the issue?*

Yes, he was told.

But he felt it couldn't be done. Not with any integrity. And now here he was, preparing to give the most difficult speech of his life.

He didn't know what the outcome might be. So little had touched the President, he doubted that this would be any different. As for what might happen to his own political career, now that he was publicly breaking with the party line – well, he told himself, he'd be around to find out.

He'd burn that bridge when he got to it.

CHAPTER ONE

The announcement was written on a sheet of paper bearing the letterhead of the American Automobile Manufacturers Association.

Dear Folks: Well, by now most of you have had the really big news, but for those who haven't, Willard Mitt Romney arrived at Ten AM March 12th...A couple of years ago, the Doctor told Lenore that her condition would not permit her to have another child and that she would have to undergo a major operation. However, she had a lot of faith... After delivery, the Doctor said, "I don't see how she became pregnant, or how she carried the child." He may not understand, but we do. We consider it a blessing for which we must thank the Creator of all.

On the ides of March, 1947, George and Lenore Romney brought their newest boy home to meet his older siblings. He had been christened Willard Mitt – in the first instance, named for J. Willard

Marriott, an old family friend – at the time, Marriott was a businessman running a chain of family-style restaurants, but by the mid-fifties, he would establish the first Marriott Hotel. The baby's middle name, Mitt, was in honor of his father's cousin, Milton "Mitt" Romney, who had been a quarterback for the Chicago Bears years before his namesake was born. Laden with family and personal history, the infant's name was quickly shortened to a family-approved nickname – Billy.

Margo, Jane, and Scott gathered around the bassinet to look down on the newest member of the family. The youngest of them, Scott, was already six years old; all three of the Romney children were looking forward to having another to play with.

The family was a close-knit unit. George Romney was forty years old when the youngest of his children was born; though a person of serious personal convictions and undeniable focus, he also had a booming laugh and a strong physical presence that seemed to draw the attention of everyone around him. He had strong genes, too; his children, especially the youngest, would grow up to look a great deal like their father.

The children's mother, Lenore LaFount Romney, had enjoyed a brief career as a stage and film actress before marrying George – in Hollywood during the Thirties, she had picked up parts in films with Greta Garbo and Jean Harlow, and as animated films and talkies entered the picture, her theater training led to voice-over roles, such as "speaking" dogs and cats. George's seven-years-long courtship of her had been indefatigable, even when she left him behind for a time to pursue her career. He would later recount it as the greatest "sales achievement" of his own business career.

The two had common roots, both being raised in multi-generational Mormon families with family ties to the early foundation of the church in the 1800s. George had been born in a Mexican Mormon colony – founded to preserve the practice of polygamy, as it was illegal in the United States – to two missionaries; Lenore's father had converted to the Church of Latter-Day Saints in his home country of England, before moving to the United States decades before she was born. Their four children, too, were raised devoutly Mormon, and the church formed a pillar of Romney's life as he grew up, even playing a part in his political career later down the line.

From the beginning, Romney was close with both of his parents. As the last in the lineup, he enjoyed more attention from both of them than his older siblings had; their father was "more settled" at that point in his life, according to one of Romney's sisters. His father was described as a man who was constantly busy, always on the move; he liked to send out bulletins to family and friends to let them know what he was up to, and his youngest was a frequent player in the letters. "[Billy is] bold and inclined to be a bit reckless - loves to climb up on high chairs and say, 'Careful, careful, careful!'...took him to visit Santa Claus, and he walked right up like a man and shook hands!"

It was around the time that little Billy Romney entered kindergarten that he made a decision about his moniker, telling first his teacher and fellow students that he wanted to be called Mitt. Though it was a harder sell at home – it's difficult to change a child's name when you've called them something for the first five years of their life – eventually his determination won over, and Mitt stuck with Romney for the rest of his life, along with hundreds of questions, over the years, about what it was short for. *Mitchell? Michael? Milton?* Being able to tell his classmates that he was named after his famous football star cousin eased the teasing that might otherwise have ensued.

For the first several years of his life, Romney lived with his family in Detroit, Michigan. George Romney worked for the American Automobile Manufacturers Association; during World War II, he had served as the main spokesman for the auto industry, and worked along with others in the industry to form a cooperative arrangement that would benefit all companies who opted in to share their insights into improvements in production. George was known as a savvy businessman; his big personality played a part, as he was able to convince those around him to take his point of view as their own. In 1953, when Romney was eight years old and his siblings in their mid to late teens, George moved the family from the city of Detroit to the wealthy, peaceful, beautiful suburbs of Bloomfield Hills. Soon after, George accepted the role of CEO and chairman of American Motors; the company had been struggling, and George was brought on board to turn the struggle into profitability.

With his experience and the weight that his dynamic personality carried, that's exactly what George did. A series of executive decisions enabled the company to avoid bankruptcy; other decisions gradually led American Motors out of the darkness of financial instability and into the light of profitable returns. It also resulted in profitable returns for George personally; his family's wealth climbed immeasurably during this time, and considering that George had come from a poor family and had frequently been broke throughout his younger life, the change marked an almost unprecedented move to privilege. Watching his father step in to rescue the floundering company from its own mistakes, some of Romney's earliest memories were of the power of taking charge: standing up, making decisions, and leading others.

If the father could do it, Romney began to believe, then so could the son.

Though Romney looked a great deal like his father,

his temperament was more closely aligned with his mother's: even and calm, rather than dynamic and intense. Still, it was his father that he idolized. As a child, while his schoolmates dreamed of becoming movie stars, athletes, and the president, Romney pictured himself running a car company, just like his father.

His rather cautious temperament made him unique among his siblings; his father, leading family discussions, would receive a chorus of enthusiastic approval from the older three, countered – as remembered by Romney's siblings – by a careful, noncommittal, "Well, have you thought about this?" from the youngest.

Romney's early years were marked by privilege, but not of the sort that made his life outrageously different from the norm. The family lived in a comfortable, roomy suburban home; he grew accustomed to seeing his father appear at public events, be interviewed on television, and even take the lead in advertising spots, some appearing on the Disneyland television show. In 1959, George was the focus of a cover article in Time Magazine. Each new appearance, each new recognition, only caused Romney's idolization of George to grow. His father, he was convinced, could do no wrong; he was, as Romney would later state, "the definition of a successful human." George and Lenore, opposite in terms of personality and approach, often bickered amongst themselves, but their marriage stood the test of time and on the whole, the Romney family remained united under George's headship, much like the company he ran.

In the seventh grade, George and Lenore enrolled their youngest son in Cranbrook School, a private prep academy not far from their home in Bloomfield Hills. It was undoubtedly an environment vastly different from the public schools he had attended up until then; a privileged child himself, he found himself surrounded by peers with even more privilege, more wealth, more power behind their family names. Romney was somewhat intimidated by this, but he did his best to shake it off, and made a few friends as quickly as he could.

In the surroundings of his new school, his laid-back, even, cautious temperament came to the fore. Excellence was prized among his classmates, but Romney was not a young man to whom excelling came naturally. Even at home, playing "to-the-death" tennis matches with his older siblings, he was quick to give up in the face of their more advanced athleticism; at school, his diffident approach to sports meant that he was more or less a bystander in the heat of any match.

One classmate recalled a particularly memorable time when Romney was a competitor in a 2.5-mile race that was held at halftime during a football game. By the time the second half of the game started, all of the runners had returned, with the glaring exception of Romney, who didn't show up until a good ten minutes after the previous straggler. He made it to the finish line – albeit collapsing twice along the way – and garnered cheers from the audience when he finally completed the race and the football game was allowed to continue.

On the other hand, if he didn't have much to give in the way of athletic pursuits, he was at least even-handed, even bipartisan, in his scholastic endeavors, too: "He can do a lot better," his teachers wrote disapprovingly on his report cards. "He wastes too much time in class." The general consensus was that Romney was a bright boy with potential who simply didn't care enough to apply himself. In just about everything in his life, he adhered strictly to the middle of the road.

What he did apply himself to was having a good time – but not in a party-forward sort of way. Romney's idea of fun was to pull pranks, many of them harmless – some less so. He would engage in "ice blocking," sliding down the hills at the local golf course on a large block of ice; one such episode led to him being detained by the police, along with his girlfriend, Ann Davies. On one memorable occasion, he staged a full formal dinner on the concrete berm in the middle of a major street. As high school progressed and everyone got their first cars – or at least were old enough to borrow their parents' cars – most of his classmates took up the ever-popular hobby of parking; Romney would dress in a police uniform and bang on the windows, startling his friends into thinking they were in trouble. Towards the end of his high school years, Romney was involved in a "prank" that, as he later said, "went too far," holding down a younger student and forcibly cutting short the boy's hair.

Despite the enjoyment he derived from pranks, school, in general, was not a preferred activity for Romney. Around the time that he was fourteen, his father announced his intention to run for the office of governor of Michigan. Delighted by the chance to spend more time with the man he loved more than anyone else, Romney happily took George up on his request that his youngest son work on his campaign. Romney's job was to take over the booths that were set up at local events, adorned with a "Romney for Governor" banner. Armed with a loudspeaker, he would shout to the public, "You should vote for my father for Governor. He's a truly great person. You've got to support him. He's going to make things better!"

George's bid for governor was successful, and by the time Romney was sixteen, he was enjoying slightly elevated status in school as the Governor's son. It potentially counterbalanced any social ostracism that he might have otherwise faced as one of the very few Mormon boys in the school; in terms of how his religion impacted him in school, he would later say, "I think it's a helpful thing for the development of the character of a young person to be different from their peers. It's a blessing to be different and stand up for that," although he also admitted, "My faith was not a burden to me. I didn't smoke and I didn't drink, and that was about it."

During the second half of his high school career, Romney continued to seek out closeness with his father by working as an intern in the Governor's office in the summers. He took up the same general position as he had occupied in family debates, injecting an occasional, "Have you thought about this?" during discussions on policy. A friend of his father's who also worked in the office recalled ruefully, "Sometimes you'd think, 'That kid ought to shut up!' But he was always nice to be around."

Despite the apparently inherent lukewarm nature of Romney's school pursuits, he didn't shy away from spreading himself around; by his senior year, he was helping to manage the ice hockey team and belonged to about a dozen school clubs. He was reasonably popular and well-liked, though he was not seen as a leader in any capacity.

A few months before graduation, he began to date Ann Davies, a friend who attended Cranbrook's sister school, Kingswood; the two would continue their relationship after graduation. Romney's father George appeared at his son's graduation from Cranbook, delivering a speech in which he told the crowd of nearly eighty graduating boys, "If the girl you're interested in doesn't inspire you to greater effort than you would undertake without knowing her, then you'd better look around and get another." The wife they chose, he told them, would have a larger part in shaping their lives than any other person. What George didn't know at the time was that a few days before, during prom, Romney had already proposed to Ann, and the two were officially engaged. With his father's advice ringing in his ears, Romney was certain that he'd made the right choice.

In the final year of school at Cranbrook, with the prospect of college looming large, Romney doubled down on his scholastic endeavors and worked hard to improve his grades, finally managing to at least escape the rut of "middle of the road" grades if not exactly reaching the excellence that his teachers believed he was capable of. In 1965, he said goodbye to Cranbrook; his yearbook photo shows a clear-eyed young man with a half-smile that seems to suggest he knew he *could* have done better – but that might have interfered with all the fun he was having.

CHAPTER TWO

C alifornia's Stanford University was the next stop on Mitt Romney's educational journey. In the fall of 1965, freshly engaged to Ann Davies, he left his family home further behind than ever before and took up residence for a year on the campus.

Academics continued not to be a thing of much personal interest to Romney, and he continued to be somewhat middle-of-the-road; in the time period and the environment in which he came to California, he was far from alone in this lack of interest. The middle of the Sixties saw the rise of the counter-culture movement in California's Bay Area, with marches and sit-ins for civil rights campaigns turning into regular occurrences on the local streets. At the same time, the involvement of the United States in the Vietnam War was leading to increased outspokenness by many members of those movements; cultural and political protests were part of the lifeblood of the area. Romney, despite being raised by a family with strong political views, held himself more or less aloof from the goings on around him, refusing to get caught up in counter-culture. He counted himself as an independent. He wouldn't side with those who were against involvement in the Vietnam War, instead voicing his reserved support for it and what he saw as the necessity for American involvement – though he would repeatedly request and receive multiple deferments so he himself did not have to fight. In the spring of 1966, a counter-culture group of anti-war activists staged a sit-in at the administrative offices of Stanford, demonstrating against draft status tests; the only protest that Romney joined during his time at Stanford was a counter-protest against the protestors.

In the summer of 1966, Romney left Stanford – and the United States – behind when he was given an assignment as a Mormon missionary. It was a tradition in the church, and especially in his family: George and his two brothers, as well as Romney's own older brother Scott, had all served their time as missionaries, and so had Romney's grandfather and great-grandfather before him. For a short time, Romney had considered bucking the tradition and remaining at Stanford, where he had already been accepted for sophomore membership by the Phi Kappa Sigma fraternity – in the end, his unwillingness to disappoint his father and go against the family won out, and he shipped out for Le Havre, France.

His time as a missionary constituted Romney's first real brush with discomfort and rejection. In the sparsely-appointed and crowded missionary home he shared with his fellows, he quickly found that the work of spreading the word was challenging, even demoralizing; for the first time, he felt, "most of what I was trying to do was rejected," by those he tried to speak to. He also found himself confronted with challenges to his beliefs, and not just his religious ones, either; the French people often brought up the issue of American involvement in Vietnam, and Romney debated them hotly, defending what he saw as necessity, just as he had done back in Stanford. During this time, a 4-D ministerial deferment protected him from serving in the armed forces.

Still, stubbornness was an asset in the field, and Romney had a certain amount of that quality innate to his personality, inherited from both sides. Within about a year after his arrival in Le Havre, he was called to Paris to serve as assistant to the mission president, H. Duane Anderson. The living circumstances in Paris were vastly different from those he'd endured as a humble missionary; the president and his staff were housed in a mansion.

At twenty-one years old, as assistant to the chief overseer of the French mission, one of Romney's duties was to drive church officials to the congregations all over France. On one such journey, in June 1968, Romney's car was struck head-on by a Mercedes driven by a Catholic priest who had lost control of his speeding car and swerved into the other lane. One of Romney's passengers died from the crash; Romney and the others were injured and woke up in the hospital. The woman who had died was the wife of Anderson, the mission president; Anderson, heart-broken, flew back to the United States to bury his wife, leaving Romney to step in as co-president to help pick up the pieces of the disorganized mission. He remained in France until December 1968; by the end of his tenure, he was in a position of oversight and received recognition for his work to organize and streamline procedures. For the first time, he had the opportunity to showcase how he had inherited more than just his father's looks – but also his ability to turn a distressed organization around and head it in the other direction.

While Romney was out of the country, his girlfriend and fiancée Ann Davies had decided to convert to the LDS church in order to marry him when he returned. Still, their engagement had been on hold for a long time, some thirty months – when he came back to the States, they met up to discuss whether their affection had withstood the long time apart, and if marriage was still the right thing to do. They decided that it had, and it was. Three months after his return, in March 1969, they were married in a civil ceremony in Bloomfield Hills. Like most Mormon unions, it was a "double wedding" of a sort; in order to be recognized and sanctified by the church, they flew to Utah the next day for another wedding ceremony in the Salt Lake City Mormon Temple.

Ann was attending Brigham Young University in Provo, Utah. Rather than return to Stanford, as he had considered doing, Romney decided to join his new wife there. The two rented a basement apartment as they continued their studies; their first child, Taggart, was born a year after their marriage, and suddenly Romney was juggling not only college but also marriage and fatherhood. It was almost a shock to the system, after the rather free and easy life he'd led through most of his young adulthood; however, after a few years wrangling his role as a missionary, perhaps it wasn't as far from his comfort zone as it might have been otherwise. Like his father, Romney struggled at times to balance his home life with other business pursuits, but he loved his wife and quickly fell in love with his newborn son. Balance was a challenge, but he was determined to do right by his growing family, just as he felt his own parents had done right by him.

While Romney had been focused on other things in France, the anti-war movement that he had opposed while he was at Stanford had been growing. In the time that he was overseas, his father had thrown his hat into the ring as a potential presidential candidate for the 1968 election; the goal was admirable, as was everything George did in the eyes of his son. George's campaign failed, but Romney was shocked to find, upon returning home, that an integral part of it had been involvement in the same anti-war movements that he had stayed strictly out of while in California. Romney had been defending US involvement in Vietnam even to the people of France who had argued against it; to come back and find that his father, the person that he had always looked up to the most, had apparently disagreed with his own privately-held notions threw him for a loop.

George was then working for the Nixon Administration, serving in the cabinet as the Secretary of Housing and Urban Development. His political career had not gone as far as he had hoped, but he was determined to make the best of it and do what he could for the American people. Far from having his faith in his father shaken, Romney's trust in George was so devout that, instead, he found himself questioning his own beliefs. In 1970, when Romney was interviewed for a profile of the children of serving members of the cabinet, Romney's view was much more closely aligned with those of his father. US involvement in Vietnam was misguided, he opined, going so far as to state, "If it wasn't a political blunder to move into Vietnam, I don't know what is."

Spending his days in class and his evenings and weekends as a married father of a small child – and then another; his second son, Matthew, was born in 1971 – Romney began to apply himself more fully to his educational goals. He no longer had time for pranks; they had served as a way to distract himself from his lack of focus in other areas, but now that they were in his past, he filled his time with more important things. In his senior year at BYU, his family's political aspirations expanded when his mother decided to run for Senate. He took time off from school to support her, joining her campaign even as he had done for his father's, taking on the role of driver as he had done for the mission and piloting his mother across all 83 counties in Michigan. Lenore's push for the Senate ended in defeat; still, through his work on his mother's behalf, Romney gained more experience in the political field, an experience that would serve him well later on.

When Romney graduated from Brigham Young University in 1971, he had a GPA of 3.97, a marked increase from his previous scholastic record, and a clear indication of the fact that he was at last starting to settle down and apply himself, as his teachers from high school had so wished he would. He delivered the commencement address to the university, honing his speechifying skills at the same time as he clutched his hard-won BA in English to his chest.

Romney's next goal was a business degree, with his father's example in mind. But George himself advised his youngest son to take another direction; law school, he pointed out, would furnish a valuable addition to his career, even if he never pursued the actual practice of law. A law degree was a common background for many political candidates; with both of his parents having political experience under their belts, it was likely that Romney himself would pursue the political arena on at least some level. Romney took his father's advice, while still balancing it with his own goals; Harvard Law and Harvard Business had recently created a joint program coordinating the necessary classes for a Juris Doctor/Master of Business Administration degree, and Romney selected this four-year program as his next step forward.

While at Harvard, Romney stayed out of direct involvement in politics, choosing again to focus on getting as close to excellence in his studies as he had ever managed. The data-driven, case study methodologies used by his professors appealed to the logical, step-by-step way his brain tended to work; between the dedicated application of his energies and the serendipity of a learning environment that seemed tailored to his needs and interests, Romney did extremely well throughout his four years at Harvard. One of his professors at Harvard Law was Alan Dershowitz; years later, when Dershowitz was serving as an attorney for

Donald Trump, Romney would recall his professor's tendencies as a teacher and use his prior experience as part of his basis for the stand he would take on some of the most divisive political issues of his career.

In 1975, Romney graduated cum laude from Harvard Law, ranking in the top third of his class; his graduation from Harvard Business put him in the top five percent, naming him a Baker Scholar. It had taken more than twenty years, but Romney finally appeared to be living up to the potential that his high school teachers had suspected lay somewhere deep within.

CHAPTER THREE

Fresh out of Harvard, with a wife and three small children – his third, Joshua, was born in 1975 – Romney quickly passed the Michigan bar exam, but decided to stick to his original plan of pursuing a career in business, as his father had. His name and reputation earned him the attention of several large firms. In the end, he decided to join Boston Consulting Group, hoping that the experience of consulting across a variety of companies would better equip him to later take on CEO and management positions.

Romney did well in consulting, and ended up staying in the field for the majority of his business career, rather than taking executive office in a single company as he had originally assumed he would do. In 1977, he joined Bain and Company, another consulting firm. Bain and Company was a stake planter; rather than make recommendations to its clients before walking away, it would come in, make recommendations, and assist in implementing them until the job was finished. It was a higher investment of time and effort – and a more direct level of responsibility for the outcome of the firm's recommendations. At thirty years old, Romney struck his colleagues as confident well beyond his age. Within a year of onboarding with Bain and Company, he was named vice president, and quickly became one of the firm's most in-demand consultants, even above some who had years longer experience in the field.

There was more of a demand than ever on Romney's time; still, he did his best to maintain the balance that was required to keep his family happy. As VP at Bain and Company, he was a big earner; added to his family's already not-inconsiderable wealth and privilege, Romney seemed to fit the typecasting of all-American big-business executive. On the weekends and his rare vacations, he packed up his kids, wife, and dog in the car and drove to holiday spots across the country; one such occasion would later come back to feature in his political career, as what one reporter called "[Romney] critics' best friend."

In the early eighties, Romney stepped sideways as co-founder and president of a spin-off endeavor, Bain Capital. Rather than consulting on established companies regarding management, Bain Capital was a venture capital concern. Romney put veto power in the hands of the partners, arranging matters so that any one partner who saw damaging holes in potential investment proposals could call a halt. Romney was the foremost among them in exercising this power; through the first year of Bain Capital's existence, he saw so many faults that only a small handful of investments slipped through.

Finding the faults in investment possibilities turned out to be his strong point; the few investments that he brought into the firm on his own often failed to be winning propositions. Not long after Bain's launch, Romney pushed the company to focus more on leveraged buyouts rather than startups. Though Bain Capital was far from a complete success with this move, overall the business saw a worthwhile return on initial investments, working with companies like Domino's Pizza, Sealy, Artisan Entertainment, and Sports Authority. The practice of leveraged buyouts was a gamble in which the everyday employees often lost; changing the structure of a company to return it to solvency or to avoid bankruptcy often meant laying off thousands of workers. The analysis was data driven, a trait at which Romney excelled at, as his own approach to things was largely based on logic and numbers, rather than giving attention to the real people who might be affected. It was not a business in which soft hearts could succeed.

Meanwhile, Bain and Company were coming into their own troubled waters. In 1991, Romney agreed to return as the new CEO, while still acting as managing partner at Bain Capital. Rescuing Bain and Company from the jaws of bankruptcy meant a lot of convincing – working with creditors to accept less than full payment in the interests of receiving payment at all, talking Bain and his co-founders into returning money they had borrowed from the company, and restructuring the employee stock-ownership arrangement to increase financial transparency and in-reach funds. Within a year, following in his father's footsteps, Romney had turned Bain and Company around and set it back on its path of financial solvency. By this point, Bain and most of his co-founders had left the firm for greener pastures; Romney organized an election for a new leadership team, handed the keys over to them, and returned to Bain Capital.

But his time at Bain Capital, too, was gradually coming to an end. In the early 1990s, Romney had started to think about what might lay ahead for him – not just in the business world, but in the political sphere. He knew that his father expected him to follow in his footsteps, parlaying business success into at least a stint in office. His mother, too, had laid the groundwork for him. As the 1994 Senate race grew closer, and he observed the rocky ground upon which the incumbent Senator stood, he wavered on whether now was the time to make his move – it was his wife Ann who made the decision for him, urging him to run.

Up until 1993, Romney had registered as an

Independent; in the 1992 presidential primaries, he voted for Paul Tsongas, a former senator from Massachusetts who also happened to be a Democrat. The political environment surrounding the senate race in Massachusetts seemed tailor-made for an upset; incumbent Ted Kennedy was seeking his sixth term, but the Democratic Congress as a whole was unpopular at the time, and Kennedy himself had suffered a blow to his reputation via a recent highly-publicized rape trial against his nephew, William Kennedy Smith. Commentators and pundits saw Kennedy as vulnerable to opposition; a new face in the race would have half his work done for him.

Romney decided to be that new face.

In October of 1993, he changed his party affiliation to Republican; four months later, in February 1994, he announced his candidacy for the senate seat. He was far from the only one who decided to step in, but Romney was an extremely effective fundraiser, which went a long way to helping him be one of the main threats to Kennedy. His platform presented him as a solid, all-American businessman who had created more than ten thousand jobs in his relatively brief career; "Ultimately," Romney told his audience, "this is a campaign about change."

Kennedy wasn't about to throw in the towel. He attacked Romney's shifting positions on matters such as abortion – an issue that would continue to cause division among Romney's adherents throughout his political career – and highlighted the mass layoffs that had resulted from Romney's work through Bain Capital. It was the layoffs, compared to his claims about creating thousands of jobs, that stuck most painfully in the craw of Massachusetts voters. Romney ran hard, but he ultimately lost the race.

The loss was hard to stomach. The day after the votes were in, Romney quietly went back to his job at Bain Capital, telling his brother. "I never want to run for something again unless I can win."

CHAPTER FOUR

T he next few years saw a number of personal challenges in Romney's life – and more tragedies than he had ever had to face up until then.

The first was one of the hardest blows. In 1995, his father, George, succumbed to a heart attack. George had been out of the public eye for some time, but he had stayed active to the last, taking part in volunteer organizations, even meeting with a group the night before his death. Throughout Romney's senate run, George had been right there with him for every move, even temporarily coming to stay in his son's house to give him advice and support; just as Romney had campaigned on his father's behalf, George took up the torch on behalf of his son.

Losing his idol, the touchstone of his entire life, the man he looked up to and modeled his career after, was a devastating loss for Romney. It was made worse when, a few years later, the physical symptoms that Ann had been manifesting for some time returned a diagnosis of multiple sclerosis. Without his father there to support and guide him, Romney felt at a loss. Losing his father had been almost impossible for him, emotionally; hearing his wife be diagnosed with such a serious illness was "the worst day of [his] life."

The next year, Romney also lost his mother, Lenore, in the aftermath of a grievous stroke.

Suddenly, the idea of balance was no longer a question of managing his family and his business. There were more important things at stake, he realized. The first priority was to take care of Ann – though the first few years after her diagnosis were difficult and painful, she was able to develop a therapeutic routine that enabled her to live as normal a life as possible, without many of the limitations usually posed by the disease. With her health stabilized, Ann encouraged Romney to accept a new job opportunity that had come his way – a position of oversight in the organization which was responsible for the upcoming 2002 Winter Olympics, to be held in Salt Lake City, Utah.

The position bore marked similarities to others he'd held over the years. The organization was in something of a shambles; it needed to be re-structured, with better management of the financial aspects moving forward, or it risked failing to bring the Olympics to reality at all; at the time that Romney took over, it was something shy of 400 million dollars below its intended revenue goal. There were also allegations of bribery at top levels. Romney pitched in with a will, restructuring budgets and boosting fundraising efforts – a job for which he had already proven his suitability. He did well in that capacity, with a persona that seemed wholesome, honest, and relatively smooth, more of a throwback to a cardigan-wearing college kid from the Fifties than anything else. His genial demeanor didn't keep him from a markedly aggressive approach to finding funds; he lobbied Congress and federal agencies so successfully and relentlessly that $400 to $600 million dollars of a $1.3 billion dollar budget came from federal funding, setting a record for government funding of an Olympic event.

At the same time, some of those who worked with Romney in the staging organization stated that things weren't as dire as Romney had represented them to begin with, and opined that Romney had seen the issue as a chance to propel himself into the limelight. The committee chair said, "It was obvious that he had an agenda larger than just the Olympics."

Whatever the case, Romney quickly became the public face of the cause of "rescuing" the Olympics. At the same time, the role granted him further first-hand experience in working along with federal and state agencies, as well as more in-depth experience with large-scale fundraising – which would come in handy a few years later. It also lent him a public persona which he had been sorely lacking – and, planned or not, created an opportunity for him re-launch his political career from the platform of being publicly perceived as a white knight.

In 2002, he left Bain Capital for good and turned his attention back to the political arena, throwing himself into the Massachusetts gubernatorial race.

Romney ran as a political outsider rather than focusing on his party affiliation; he told his audience that he viewed himself as moderate with progressive leanings. He leaned heavily on his experience as a "rescuer" – of businesses, organizations, and, when necessary, he was certain he could rescue the government, too. His track record of fiscal successes spoke loudly to most of his audience; at the same time, those same successes were part of a history that was, on the whole, rather equivocal. The image that had damned him in the senate race – a big businessman focused on his own fortunes rather than thinking of the little people he might be crushing underfoot along the way – crept out to face him once more.

Romney's campaign for governor of Massachusetts was marked by some interesting choices that well illustrated how his brain operated: logic and numbers, as opposed to the deeper meanings behind why humans do what they do, and why they think what they think. The problem of his image was a vivid example. Fighting against the public's perception of him as a faceless, heartless suit, a series of television spots centered on the "normal guy" Mitt Romney, engaging in "work days" to show how down to earth he was as he hauled garbage, herded cows, baled hay, and went fishing. The TV ads backfired on him, meeting with public disapproval rather than earning him a new group of converts, although whether this was from the tone-deaf staging of "work days" for a millionaire or the fact that he often appeared shirtless is up for debate.

Regardless of the public's amused reaction to his attempt to engage with the common man, Romney still managed to snag governorship by a five percent margin.

Romney seemed to approach governing Massachusetts as he approached everything in his business life – with caution, ready to pick holes in proposed investments, and yet with the idea that he could white-knight his way into political approval. He focused his efforts on the financials; cutting spending and closing corporate tax loopholes, he brought the state deficit up to a surplus over his tenure. He also worked on reforming health care, introducing "Romneycare," seeking to provide health care to everyone in his state. This, he believed, was the best way that he could help people. The legislature he introduced for these measures was the first of its kind in the United States, serving as Romney's main achievement during his time in office.

Despite that, Romney's approval numbers were not what he might have wished; starting off at 61 percent approval in his first year, the numbers had declined to 34 percent by his last. As he approached the end of his term as governor, he had a decision to make: where would he go next with his political career? For there seemed to be no question now about going back into the private sector. He spoke with his wife and children regarding the dilemma; his father's absence was felt more keenly than ever, but he hoped that the decision he made would have made his father proud.

On the day before he left office as governor of Massachusetts, Romney registered to campaign for another office – that of the President of the United States.

CHAPTER FIVE

Romney's campaign for president in the 2008 election was not a great success. He matched the typecasting for a presidential candidate: hair slicked back, square jaw, wide smile, middle-aged white man. But somehow, the same issue continued to plague him, and he found it difficult to connect with people on a meaningful level; political commentator and journalist Evan Thomas wrote that Romney "came off as a phony, even when he was perfectly sincere."

In the end, Romney put his own campaign on the back burner and threw his weight behind John McCain, who became the Republican presidential candidate. McCain had lambasted Romney throughout the Republican debates, calling attention to what McCain viewed as "flip-flopping," changing his position on issues as it became politically expedient. Romney objected to this – "I've been as consistent as human beings can be," he would state – although there were documented examples in which he had done just that. However, McCain now told Romney that he was on the shortlist for running mate. In the end, however, McCain went with Sarah Palin.

Romney didn't like the taste of losing anymore this time around; however, he had matured since the days when he'd told his brother that he wouldn't enter any race that he couldn't be sure of winning. When the next presidential election came around, he threw his hat in the ring once more. For many observers, this was a foregone conclusion; as Scott McLean, a professor of political science, stated, "He's really been running for president ever since the day after the 2008 election."

This time, Romney was the clear front-runner. He again launched from the platform of America needing a financial "rescue," which he was well-placed to provide. As if in proof, he raised more than fifty million dollars in the first year of his campaign, more than twice the amount of any other Republican candidate; for once, he refrained from sinking his own money into his campaign. The race ebbed and flowed, but in the end, Romney became the first member of the Mormon church to be a nominated Republican presidential candidate.

Taking that position opened Romney up to increased attacks and muck-raking from his past. In particular, there was the question of Seamus, the

Romney family dog; years before, on a long family road trip, Romney had put the Irish setter in a specially-built crate with a windshield to ride on top of the family car. Digging this episode up caused a backlash from animal lovers and political opponents alike; Newt Gingrich formulated a series of attack ads specifically based on the decades-old story. Suddenly, everyone was up in arms over Seamus, seeing Romney's treatment of the family pet as an indication of his moral character. "The issues of character are important in this election," Republican hopeful Rick Santorum told reporters. "We need to look at all those issues and make a determination as to whether that's the kind of person you want to be president of the United States."

Looking back on it from the vantage point of everything that happened in the ensuing ten years, such arguments appear almost quaint. At the time, however, they caused inexplicable damage to Romney's campaign. At the same time, for those willing to look past the pro-Seamus uproar, the story provided a foothold on Romney's approach to everything from his beliefs to his politics. As journalist Neil Swidey wrote, the story of Seamus and the family road trip "always struck me as a valuable window into how Romney operates. In everything the guy does, he functions on logic, not emotion."

Seamusgate was unexpectedly problematic for Romney, but it was far from the nail in the coffin.

During an interview with Wolf Blitzer, Romney spoke up about Russia, calling the country "our number one geopolitical foe." This, again, caused an uproar that appears almost laughably ironic from the vantage point of the future, but at the time Romney was raked over the coals for being "breathtakingly off target" in his "Cold War mentality."

What came back to haunt him the most, however, was a statement he made during an address to his supporters. "There are 47 percent of the people who will vote for [President Obama] no matter what. 47 percent who are with him, who are dependent upon government, who believe that they are victims, who believe the government has a responsibility to care for them, who believe that they are entitled to healthcare, to food, to housing, to you-name-it. These are people who pay no income tax... My job is not to worry about those people. I'll never convince them they should take personal responsibility and care for their lives."

For a man who repeatedly struggled with the public's perception of him as someone out of touch with the common man, the "47 percent" comment was almost groan-inducing. It was ironic during the actual event of the election to find that, in the end, Romney had received exactly 47 percent of the popular vote; Barack Obama had received 51.

Despite the gaffes and stumbles, Romney had been

convinced that the election was going in his favor, and was "shell-shocked" by the outcome, according to reports. Still, he recognized that the people had spoken, and in his concession speech, noted that "[Running mate Paul Ryan and I] have given our all to this campaign. I so wish that I had been able to fulfill your hopes to lead this country in a different direction, but the nation chose another leader."

His presidential aspirations were stopped cold again – but it didn't stop him from wanting what he couldn't quite achieve. The next year, he quietly admitted to an interviewer, "It kills me not to be there, not to be in the White House doing what needs to be done."

Disheartened, Romney stepped out of the public eye, returning to "normal life" – going back home every night to have dinner with his wife, and spending time with his five boys as they grew up. He served as director of Marriott International for a time and took on the role of executive partner group chairman for a firm founded by his oldest son. He seemed poised to return to life out of the political arena for good – but with encouragement from his wife and sons, he wasn't quite ready to give up yet.

CHAPTER SIX

etween 2012 and 2016, Romney's political involvement centered on lending his reputation and energy to campaigning for his fellow Republicans. As the next presidential election crept forward, talk began to circulate about whether or not he would give it one more try – but in the end, he decided against it.

His reputation for campaigning for those he backed led to his being scouted out by members of his party who were understandably concerned about the very vocal front-runner for the nomination – Donald Trump. Romney, too, was concerned; having decided that he would not wrestle Trump for the nomination himself, he did not shy away from speaking up about his thoughts on the matter. In early 2016, he joined the debate about Trump's refusal to release his taxes, as was customary for presidential candidates; Trump was being cagey for a reason, Romney opined, suggesting that there might be a "bombshell" in the returns. Trump responded in typical fashion, lashing out at Romney as "one of the dumbest and worst candidates in the history of Republican politics." Trump's apparent attempt to bully Romney into submission resulted in a rather un-Mitt-like response as Romney doubled down, speaking out critically of Trump in a speech at the Hinckley Institute of Politics: "Here's what I know: Donald Trump is a phony, a fraud. His promises are as worthless as a degree from Trump University. He's playing the American public for suckers. He gets a free ride to the White House, and all we get is a lousy hat. Let me put it plainly: if we Republicans choose Donald Trump as our nominee, the prospects for a safe and prosperous future are greatly diminished."

The back and forth continued, as it tends to do in the political arena. In an effort to do something about what he viewed as a serious danger to the country, Romney encouraged tactical voting among the Republican party – in short, pick a candidate, any candidate but Trump. Though there was evidence that tactical voting was engaged in, it wasn't enough to derail the Trump train; in the end, with Trump squaring off against Democratic nominee Hillary Clinton, Romney would lament, "I am dismayed at where we are now. I wish we had better choices."

When pressed on who he would support, he said that it was "a matter of personal conscience," and that rather than vote for Clinton or Trump, he would write in his wife's name; Ann, he said, would be "an ideal president." A few years later, he revealed that that was exactly what he had done.

Despite Romney's best efforts, Trump won the presidential election. Politely enough, Romney congratulated the winner, but publicly stated that he had "no regrets" regarding his anti-Trump speechifying, and refused to back down on the positions he had taken.

In 2018, Romney saw new potential for a foray into the political field when Utah's Senator Orrin Hatch announced his retirement. Hatch had served for forty-two years, making him the longest-serving Republican Senator in American history; though he was well respected, the majority agreed that it was time for a change. Romney announced his campaign in February 2018, and in June competed for the Republican nomination in a primary election against another Kennedy – State Representative Mike Kennedy, this time. Romney won the nomination, and later that year, won the Senate seat, with 62 percent of votes, over 30 percent for the Democratic nominee.

Before taking office, Romney made clear that he wasn't backing down in his criticism of the president, writing an editorial for the Washington Post that contained scathing criticisms of Trump's policies and character. His strong stance on the subject made it somewhat less surprising that, when the occasion of Trump's first impeachment arose at the end of 2019, Romney became the first Senator to vote to impeach a president of his own political party – crossing the party line in what he viewed as a matter too important for partisanship.

To some extent, Romney knew what he was in for. To take a stand against his own party opened him up to all sorts of criticism – not just from those he worked with, but from his constituents, from voters, even potentially from family and friends. Throughout his political career, Romney had been plagued by allegations of being a flip-flopper, of being too wishy-washy to stand up and make a difference. He wasn't happy about being in this position; he hadn't asked for it. But upon being forced to the precipice, he suddenly found himself being celebrated as a man who stuck to his guns. Though he certainly faced opposition for his choice, he also faced approval from some unexpected sources – the Democratic voters in Utah, for one—Republicans who had become disenchanted with Trump, for another. Even the organization Republicans for the Rule of Law ran television ads thanking Romney for his courage.

He'd spent his whole life being middle of the road. Independent. Moderate. Average grades; nothing excelling. But he also had a history of being able to take foundering prospects, turn them around, and send them off for brighter horizons.

Putting his political career in terms of his business acumen, it seemed that Romney was his own white knight, pulling himself out of ethical bankruptcy.

Romney was there on the Senate floor on the morning of January 6th, 2021, when the mob broke into the capitol building. He'd dealt with their kind of anger before – just the day before, a group had chanted, "Traitor! Traitor! Traitor!" at him as he boarded the plane to fulfill his duty as a senator. He knew who he considered to be to blame; "This is what the president has caused today, this insurrection!" he told reporters. As he was being evacuated in the scramble for safety, he yelled over his shoulder to Ted Cruz and other of his Republican colleagues, all of whom had supported Trump in his attempt to subvert the election, "This is what you've gotten, guys!"

Romney had never been a dynamic personality, not like his father. But the anger in his voice as he spoke about the riot at the capitol continued to be palpable with each statement, each interview. Few things can rile up Mitt Romney; January 6th is one of them.

On January 13th, during Trump's second impeachment trial, Romney was not the only Republican to stand up in favor of conviction. This time, far from being the lone centrist Republican amidst a host of Democrats, he was joined by six others from his party.

He knew he might still face accusations of being a traitor.

But the events that had transpired since the previous impeachment – the events that had transpired since his first objection to Trump's candidacy – only served to convince him ever more that he was in the right.

And he wasn't about to back down now.

In 2020, Romney did something that he had the opportunity to do in college, but which he had passed up: he marched with protestors.

The cause this time: Black Lives Matter. After the murder of George Floyd, with a spotlight on police brutality, the movement had garnered increasing support – support which was far from bipartisan. The BLM movement came right up to the party line and stopped there until June 7th, 2020, when Romney stepped out among the crowd and marched along with the protestors. He was the first Republican Senator to participate and show his support for the cause so publicly.

"We need a voice against racism," Romney stated during an interview. "We need many voices against racism and against brutality. We need to stand up and say that black lives matter."

Trump's response to this, disseminated via Twitter, mocked Romney for his actions. "*Tremendous sincerity, what a guy. Hard to believe, with this kind of political talent, his numbers would "tank" so badly in Utah!"*

Ironically enough, at that point, Romney was polling considerably higher in approval ratings than Trump himself.

Romney's choice to march with the BLM protestors garnered praise from both sides of the party line; he succeeded in kick-starting a conversation about why more Republicans weren't outspoken in support of the cause. But it wasn't just his party, or the Democrats, or even the people who might vote for him that Romney wanted approval from.

A few days after the march, he posted a throwback picture from the 1960s. In it, George Romney marched alongside protestors supporting civil rights.

Even though his father had long since passed away, Romney still wanted to follow in the footsteps of the man he idolized, the man he considered the greatest example of success. In gaining his father's approval, he managed to create his very own kind of legacy.

In September 2023, Romney announced that he would not seek re-election after his Senate term ends; in fact, he declared himself ready to retire, making way for the next generation.

What, precisely, that means for a famously energetic man who always seems to be looking for the next avenue of interest is yet to be seen. He could spend more time at home with his wife, Ann, whose MS has been in remission for the past several years. He could spend more time with his children and grandchildren – his five boys have given him twenty-three grandchildren and one great-grandchild, at last count – or on his fishing boat. He could go back to normal life – or what passed for normal life in the Romney family—politics, religion, hard work, and turning things around just when they seem about to crash.

But one imagines that, for a man who spent his entire life following in his father's footsteps, it would be difficult for Romney to quit now. George was active to the last, attending his final meeting with a volunteer organization the very night before he passed away. The legacy of the Romneys, whether the observer is on the political right or the political left, is at least of a family who has tried to do what is right. Whatever retirement looks like for Mitt Romney, it surely won't be the last that the American people hear from him. White-knighting is a hard hobby to give up.

Made in the USA
Las Vegas, NV
19 November 2023

81161138R00031

University Press returns with a short, intriguing biography of Mitt Romney.

Mitt Romney's life is a testament to the enduring spirit of American politics. Born in 1947 to a prominent political family, he emerged as a charismatic and capable leader in his own right. Romney's journey is one of transformation, from a successful businessman to a revered statesman.

Romney's early career at Bain & Company showcased his keen intellect and acumen for turning around struggling companies. However, it was his foray into politics that truly set him apart. Serving as the Governor of Massachusetts from 2003 to 2007, he earned a reputation for bipartisan cooperation, implementing a groundbreaking healthcare reform law that became a model for the nation.

His political ascent culminated in a run for the presidency in 2012, capturing the Republican nomination. Though he ultimately fell short, his campaign showcased his resilience and commitment to public service.

Romney's legacy continues to evolve as he remains a critical voice in American politics, known for his principled stands and willingness to reach across the aisle. His journey from corporate titan to political maverick serves as an inspiring example of the power of conviction and adaptability in the ever-changing landscape of American politics.

This short biography of Mitt Romney is a must-read, for it tells the intensely human story of a truly exceptional man who is changing the world in a way that no one else can.

ISBN 9798863786339

9000

9 798863 786339

SPELLBOUND SEDUCTION

A WIZARD LOVE STORY

G. M. FAIRY